KV-370-282

Contents

The Winns Primary School

25272

Rigby is an imprint of Pearson Education Limited, a company incorporated in England and Wales, having its registered office at Edinburgh Gate, Harlow, Essex, CM20 2JE. Registered company number: 872828

www.rigbyed.co.uk

Help and support for teachers, plus the widest range of education solutions

Rigby is a registered trademark of Reed Elsevier, Inc. licensed to Pearson Education Limited

Getting Even first published 2004

'The Magic Paintbrush' © Harcourt Education Limited 2004

'Theseus and the Minotaur' © William Bedford 2004

'The Giant's Eye' © Harcourt Education Limited 2004

Series editor: Shirley Bickler

11

10 9

Getting Even
ISBN 9780433035244

Group reading pack with teaching notes
ISBN 9780433035671

Illustrated by Liz Pyle, David Williams and Guy Redhead

Cover illustration © Andrew Pavitt

Designed by StoreyBooks

Repro by Digital Imaging, Glasgow

Printed and bound in China (CTPS/09)

The Magic Paintbrush

A Chinese Folk Tale

retold by Rosalind Kerven

illustrated by Liz Pyle

Getting Even

Long ago, when China was a great empire of
silk and gunpowder, there was a poor orphan
boy called Ma Liang.

He lived all by himself in a tumbledown,
wooden shack, and he was often lonely
and miserable.

But Ma Liang had a secret ambition: he
longed to be an artist.

He couldn't afford to buy any
artist's materials, but that didn't
stop him. He made everything he
needed for himself. His
'paintbrush' was a twig and
he drew all his pictures in the
sand. He spent long hours crouched
outside his shack, practising drawing.

Then, one night, Ma Liang had a very
strange dream.

He seemed to be walking through a land full
of peach blossom, towards an old man with a
long white beard.

"Hurry, Ma Liang," called the old man. "I want
to give you something."

In his outstretched hand he held a paintbrush.
It had a polished, moon-white handle and bristles
so fine they seemed to be spun from silk.

The old man said, "This brush was made by the gods from dragon pearls and stardust. It is their gift to you, but you must promise only to use it to help the poor people of China."

"Oh, thank you," cried Ma Liang, "I will!" His head spun with questions, but at that moment the old man vanished.

Ma Liang woke up in a cold sweat. For the rest of the night, he tossed and turned on his ragged sleeping mat, trying to work out what the strange dream meant.

As dawn broke, he noticed something glinting on the floor near his mat. Reaching out, he picked up a paintbrush with a moon-white handle – just like the one in his dream!

Ma Liang stared at it and ran his fingers down the gleaming handle. Then he leapt from his mat, mixed a handful of mud with water, dipped the brush in and painted a picture of a horse onto the bare wall of the shack.

As soon as it was finished, there was a loud *"Neigh!"*. The next moment, the horse tossed its head – and stepped out from the wall!

It had come alive!

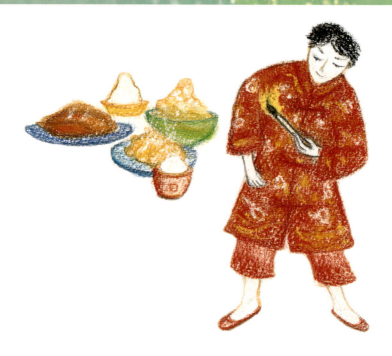

Ma Liang jumped back in fright and stared at the paintbrush. Was it... magic?

He painted more things in a fever of excitement, and every single thing became real. He painted roast duck and fried noodles and a smart new set of clothes. Laughing with happiness, he pulled on the clothes and gobbled down the delicious food.

But Ma Liang didn't forget his dream and his promise to the old man. He painted some ink and a bundle of paper scrolls. Then he jumped onto the horse and rode off into the countryside.

At every village he met poor, hungry people who were desperate for food. Ma Liang painted huge bowls of rice, vegetables and meat for them. When the food began to steam and sizzle, the people shrieked with joy. They sat down and ate until they almost burst.

11

Soon the whole of China was talking about Ma Liang and his amazing magic paintbrush. Eventually, even the wicked Emperor heard about it. He sent soldiers to hunt out Ma Liang and drag him to his palace.

"Paint me some treasure!" commanded the Emperor.

"Your Majesty," whispered Ma Liang, "I'm sorry, but I can't. I can only use this brush to help poor people."

12

"You worthless rat!" roared the Emperor. "How dare you refuse me? Unless you paint some treasure for me at once, my soldiers will cut off your head!"

Ma Liang turned white.

One of the soldiers stuck a piece of paper on the wall. "Paint me a mountain of gold!" the Emperor commanded.

So Ma Liang dipped his brush into the ink and painted with a trembling hand.

13

"What's that?" demanded the Emperor.

"Please, your Majesty, it's the sea," said Ma Liang. "And look – here's an island in the middle of it. On this island is a mountain made entirely of gold."

The picture shimmered and dissolved into a swirling mist. When it cleared, the picture had turned into an open window. Beyond it lay a beach leading down to the sea. In the distance, the sun sparkled on a golden island.

"Very clever," said the Emperor. "Now take me to this gold."

Ma Liang painted a boat – and at once it appeared in the sea, bobbing up and down on the waves.

With a whoop of greed, the Emperor hitched up his robes and leaped through the window. Then he ran down the beach and climbed on board.

"Boy!" he yelled. "Paint me the wind!"

The dark cloud of anger in Ma Liang's heart grew. He didn't want to help this greedy Emperor who already had a palace overflowing with treasure. The magic paintbrush jerked angrily in his hand – and painted a violent windstorm.

At once the storm came alive. Enormous waves rose and fell in the sea. The boat tilted,

heaved and rocked. The Emperor screamed at Ma Liang to stop it – but it was too late…

For the storm blew the boat away, right past the island and out to sea, far beyond the edge of the picture.

Where had it gone? Nobody knew, not even Ma Liang. But from that day on, the wicked Emperor was never seen again.

As for Ma Liang, he painted an enormous dragon, and when it came alive, he jumped on its back. The dragon soared into the sky and carried Ma Liang far away to a distant, secret corner of China.

There, he spent the rest of his life painting the things poor people needed, just as he had promised.

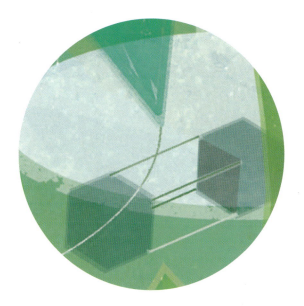

THESEUS AND THE MINOTAUR

A GREEK MYTH

retold by William Bedford

illustrated by David Williams

A long time ago, in the days of monsters and heroes, King Minos of Crete sent his son to visit Athens.

"You will enjoy yourself," King Minos told his son, "and your visit will help our kingdoms to live together in peace."

But something terrible happened. When King Minos' son arrived in Athens, he was killed by a bull.

When King Minos heard what had happened, he was wild with grief, and he wanted revenge upon the people of Athens.

"Build me a labyrinth!" he told his inventor Daedalus. "Build me a maze of twisting, turning tunnels, from which no one can escape. And at its heart, I will hide a monster: a terrible creature with razor-sharp teeth and huge jaws. It will be called the Minotaur."

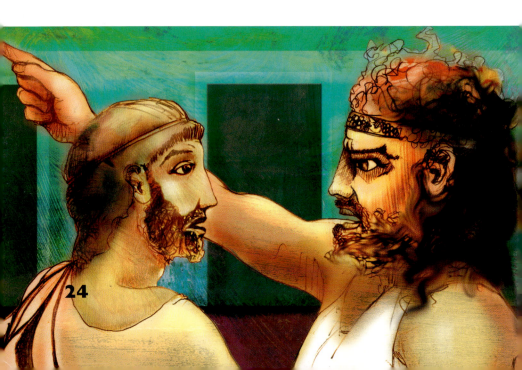

24

So Daedalus created the labyrinth. And in the darkness of the labyrinth, lurked the Minotaur.

Then King Minos put a curse on the people of Athens. "Every year, you must send me seven young girls and seven young boys," he told them. "They must enter my labyrinth and fight the Minotaur. The one who kills the Minotaur will lift the curse."

But no one ever returned from the labyrinth. Once inside, there was no escape from the all-devouring Minotaur. No ordinary human could defeat it.

25

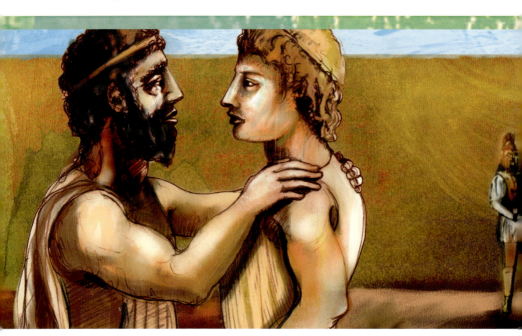

The time came again for the girls and boys to be sent to Crete. Their King, Aegeus, wept out of pity for the young Athenians who were destined to die.

Then King Aegeus' son, Theseus, stepped forward. "Let me take the place of one of these youths," Theseus said. "I will kill the Minotaur and end the curse."

Aegeus begged him not to go, but Theseus was determined. When the time came, he joined the other victims on a ship with black sails.

"If you succeed in killing the Minotaur," Aegeus told his son, "change the black sails for white ones, so that we will see the good news coming."

When they arrived on Crete, crowds were on the quays, and Ariadne, daughter of King Minos, was among them. Ariadne fell in love with Theseus as soon as she saw him. She felt pity for the brave prince who said that he wanted to be the first to go into the labyrinth.

That night, Ariadne went to see the Athenians. "I have a plan that will help you kill the Minotaur," she told Theseus. "But you must promise to help me escape afterwards. My father is a cruel man. He will have me killed if he knows that I have helped you."

Theseus listened to Ariadne's plan.

At midnight, the soldiers took Theseus to the gates of the labyrinth, and pushed him inside.

"Find your way out of there!" laughed one of the soldiers, as the gates clanked shut.

After a few moments, Theseus' eyes became used to the darkness and he took something from the folds of his cloak. It was a glimmering ball of magic thread that Ariadne had given him.

He placed the ball on the ground. Immediately, it began to unroll down the tunnel, leaving a trail of glowing thread behind it. Theseus followed, careful not to make a sound.

Suddenly, the thread led him round a corner, and there lay the Minotaur. It was asleep, but still a terrifying sight. Its great mouth was wide open, and its sharp teeth gleamed like razors in the half-light.

Theseus knew he could not kill it in a fight. His only weapon was a short dagger Ariadne had given him. His only advantage was surprise.

31

Theseus crept close to the Minotaur. Silently, he prayed to the gods. Then he took a deep breath, and yelled the Athenian war cry, "AAEEEIIIAHHHH!"

The Minotaur's eyes flew open in alarm. It struggled to its feet.

Theseus aimed the hilt of his dagger straight at the Minotaur's heart. He hit the Minotaur with all the strength he could find. The Minotaur sank backwards, stunned by the blow.

Turning the dagger round, Theseus aimed the blade straight at the creature's heart, and struck again.

"AAEEEIIIAHHHH!" he screamed. The sound echoed like a hundred warcries.

With a horrible choking gurgle, the Minotaur slumped forward. It was dead.

Theseus ran back through the labyrinth. The glowing thread led him safely to the gates, where Ariadne was waiting. When she saw him, she sobbed with relief.

In the darkness, Ariadne led Theseus and the other young Athenians back to their ship. They set sail from Crete before King Minos realised what had happened.

"You are the bravest warrior in all of Greece," Ariadne told Theseus.

"And you are the cleverest and most beautiful woman," Theseus whispered tenderly.

When they
reached the small island
of Naxos, they decided to marry.
But, as they landed on the island, the god Dionysus
spotted Ariadne and fell in love with her. He ordered
Theseus to leave Ariadne on Naxos and sail away.

Poor Theseus could not refuse Dionysus' order
and he sailed home to Athens, alone and broken-
hearted. Thinking only of Ariadne, he forgot to
change the black sails to white.

35

When King Aegeus saw his son's ship he was overjoyed. Then he saw that the sails were black. Thinking Theseus must have been killed, the old king leapt from the cliff to his death.

So Theseus succeeded in killing the Minotaur and lifted the curse from Athens. He went on to become a great king, but, in his heart, he always mourned his father and longed for Ariadne.

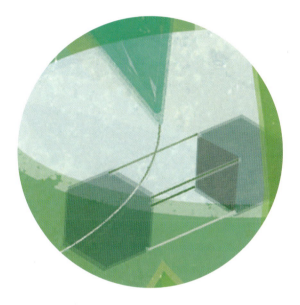

The Giant's Eye

written by Jane Langford

illustrated by Guy Redhead

Kofi's mother and father talked long into the night.

This drought will bring starvation to the whole village. Kofi might be better off in the jungle.

But the jungle is so dangerous! Wild animals stalk in the darkness!

We must try not to worry about him.

He will be all right, Mother.

I will go in the morning as the sun rises!

43

Kofi set off for the jungle. The heat of the jungle was intense.

The heart of the jungle was tangled and dark.

The sounds of the jungle were eerie.

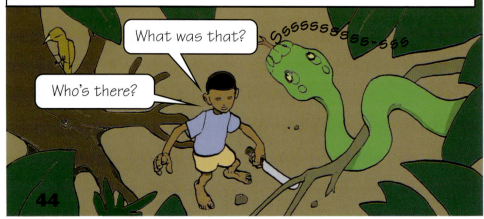

Chapter 2

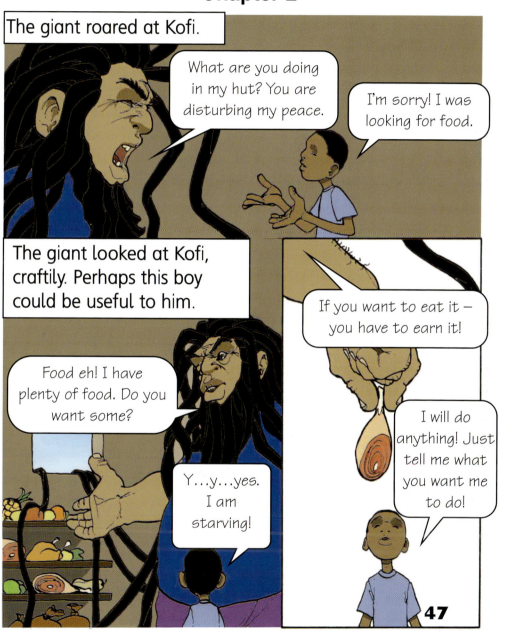

The giant roared at Kofi.

What are you doing in my hut? You are disturbing my peace.

I'm sorry! I was looking for food.

The giant looked at Kofi, craftily. Perhaps this boy could be useful to him.

If you want to eat it – you have to earn it!

Food eh! I have plenty of food. Do you want some?

Y...y...yes. I am starving!

I will do anything! Just tell me what you want me to do!

47

The giant set Kofi to work.

Many days passed and Kofi always had plenty to eat.

Kofi smiled at the giant, but he was worried about his family.

You are putting some fat on your bones at last! Don't eat too much or it will slow you down! I need you to work hard for me!

What's wrong boy?

It's my family. I'm worried about them. I want to go home and see how they are.

48

49

Kofi raced back through the jungle. He told his family about the giant.

I clean the house and cook the meals. I gather wood and carry water. I work hard for him, but he feeds me well!

This is excellent news, Kofi.

But why have you come back? We have hardly anything left to eat.

Kofi's brother and sister showed him the cracked earth and the dying crops.

The giant wants one of you to go and work for him while I am home. He will feed you as he has fed me.

I don't think the drought will ever end.

Wonderful! Brother, you must go!

We must hope that it will! But listen! I have something to tell you!

Me? Are you sure?

Kofi's brother hurried off into the jungle. Kofi returned to the hut.

Is this all the grain that is left?

Are those all the yams?

This well is nearly dry!

Kofi knew that his family would not survive for much longer.

I will go and ask the giant if he will give me some food for you.

But you are tired. Rest for a day or two and then go.

Please stay with us a while.

Kofi agreed to stay for two nights, but then he hurried back to the giant's hut.

Hello! Hello! I am back!

51

The giant was alone. He looked startled to see Kofi.

That was quick!

My family are starving! They need your help ... but where is my brother?

He went home this morning. He didn't even clean the hut before he left!

That's strange!

Kofi was puzzled by his brother's behaviour, but he put it out of his mind.

My family are starving! Please will you help them?

If you want food for your family you will have to earn it!

I will do anything!

Chapter 3

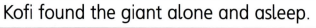

Kofi found the giant alone and asleep.

Wake up! Wake up! Where is my sister?

Zzzzzz Zzzzzz

The giant struggled to open his eyes.

What? What? What do you mean?

My sister came to work for you! Where is she?

Your sister was lazy and didn't work properly! She left yesterday.

That's not true! She's not lazy, and if she left yesterday she would have got home before I left!

56

Kofi ran crying through the jungle, back to his parents.

The whole village gathered round.

The villagers wanted to take revenge. But Kofi warned them to be careful.

As night fell, everyone crept into the jungle.

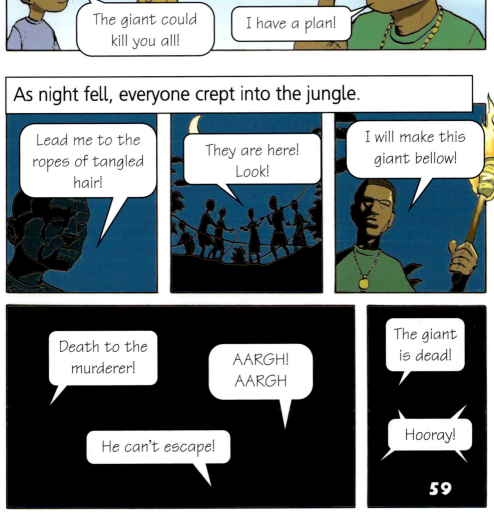

The liquid spilt onto the bones.

In his excitement, Kofi dropped the bottle.

Kofi! You've spilt it on to the giant's ashes!

Oh no! The the giant will come back to life!

Get back everyone!

Run for your lives!

But the elixir was not powerful enough to bring a whole giant back to life.

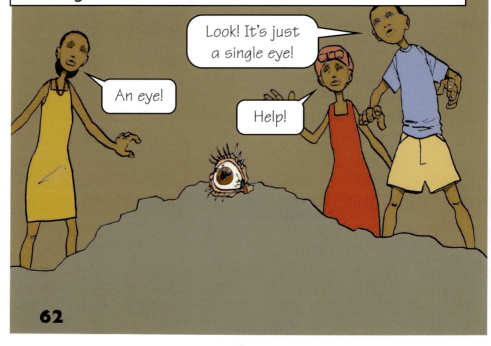

Look! It's just a single eye!

An eye!

Help!

But they weren't as safe as they thought. The giant's eye was very powerful. Every time it blinked, someone somewhere in the world died.

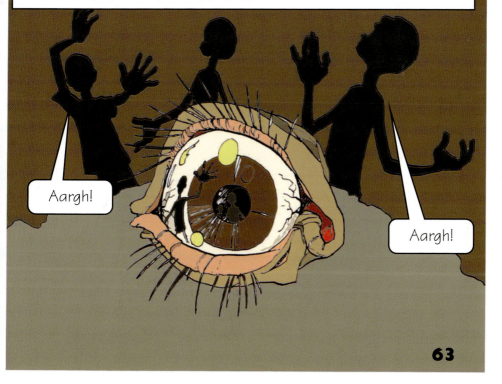

So be warned! You never know who the eye will blink for next.